Original title:
Plum Blossoms in the Air

Copyright © 2025 Creative Arts Management OÜ
All rights reserved.

Author: Amelia Montgomery
ISBN HARDBACK: 978-1-80586-331-1
ISBN PAPERBACK: 978-1-80586-803-3

Petal Constellations in the Sky

Little petals take to flight,
Dancing hard, oh what a sight!
They twirl and swirl, a floral race,
Chasing whispers through the space.

Like silly bugs on a sugar spree,
They giggle loud as they float free,
Mapping cosmos with every glide,
A constellation made with pride.

Melodies Carried by Gentle Zephyrs

The breeze hums tunes of happy cheer,
With joking gusts, it draws us near,
Twisting mustaches with a breeze,
Tickling noses like soft tease.

Sounding like a band on high,
Flutes and drums in the sky,
Laughter echoes with each gust,
As petals tumble—oh, they must!

Capturing the Essence of Soft Wind

Soft whispers sneak around the trees,
While tiny folks dance with the bees,
They grab the air like candy treats,
Twisting like spaghetti in fun beats.

Airy mischief on a whim,
As petals race and dare to swim,
Caught in laughter, in silly spins,
In the chaos, everyone wins!

Garden of Wishes Under Sunlight

In this garden where dreams thrive,
Wishes hop and jive, alive!
Bouncing balls of blooms and glow,
Tickling toes in a sunlight show.

Children giggle, try to catch,
Wishes flying—what a match!
They run in circles, laughing loud,
As wishes fly, they feel so proud.

The Soft Caress of Waking Nature

The trees stretch limbs with such grace,
As sleepy bunnies start a race.
A chirping choir sings a tune,
While squirrels plot schemes 'neath the moon.

Legs of daisies poke through the frost,
They whisper, "Hey! Don't count us lost!"
A butterfly trips over its wings,
Laughing at all the joy that spring brings.

Ephemeral Beauty in Flight

A ladybug flies, got caught in a net,
Winks at the sun, feeling quite wet.
She fluffs her spots, gives a loud pout,
"I never asked for a swim to sprout!"

The dragonflies dance, twirling in glee,
One almost crashes into a tree.
They giggle and spin, in a dizzying plight,
"Why do we fly? It just feels so right!"

Breezes Carrying Sweet Reminders

The wind whispers tales from the past,
Of flowers that bloom, oh, how they last!
It tickles my nose, then gives a loud sneeze,
Quick as a wink, it sways all the leaves.

A gust carries scent of cake in the air,
But it's only a pie, life's little snare.
With petals of pink dancing like mad,
Who needs a plan when you're feeling so glad?

A Serenade of Floral Whispers

The daisies giggle, the roses hum,
While tulips trumpet, 'Look, here we come!'
Petals prance in a colorful storm,
Each trying to show who'll get the most warm.

Next to the fence, the violets conspire,
"Is it my hat, or the sun that inspires?"
And out comes a frog in a tiny soft hat,
Croaking a tune, 'Look at me, chat!'

Fragrant Conversations of the Heart

In the garden, whispers fly,
Silly shadows dance up high.
Petals gossip, sipping dew,
Telling tales of me and you.

Bumblebees wear tiny hats,
Buzzing jokes among the chats.
Sunbeams laugh as they parade,
While butterflies play charades.

An Ode to the Blooming Horizon

Morning hues with giggles clash,
While in the breeze, the jokes make splash.
Daffodils wear socks askew,
As daisies burst in laughter, too.

The sky rolls eyes at clouds so slow,
Making faces as they flow.
Joyful sprouts can hardly wait,
For spring's big, blooming date!

Unlocking the Secrets of Spring's Canvas

Brush in hand, a painter's dream,
Colors twirl and giggles gleam.
Each stroke a joke, a laugh, a cheer,
Nature's antics, loud and clear.

Canvas wide with secrets shared,
As playful breezes run unpaired.
Sprouts confide in buzzing bees,
Creating laughs upon the breeze.

A Flutter of Petal Whispers

Petals flutter, secrets spill,
In breezy jokes, a playful thrill.
Swaying branches join the fun,
As leaves play hide with the sun.

Sipping nectar, birds retell,
The tales of blooms, oh so swell.
Giggles sprout in every fold,
Nature's humor, bright and bold.

Illuminated Paths of Nature's Brush

Colors burst like laughter's call,
A floral dance that won't let fall.
Bees doing cha-cha, what a sight!
Nature's party, pure delight!

Leaves are giggling, swaying free,
While squirrels throw a wild spree.
Petal confetti fills the air,
Who knew blooms could dance with flair?

Embracing the Rhythms of Spring

A gentle breeze with a cheeky grin,
Laughs with frogs as they hop and spin.
Buds pop open, like bags of snacks,
Nature's prankster, no time for acts!

Chirps and chirrups, a comedic band,
Beetles waltzing hand in hand.
Blossoms wink from every nook,
The whole world's gone a little kook!

Serendipity in Petals' Drift

Falling petals wear tiny hats,
Wind goes giggling past the cats.
A dainty shower, soft and bright,
Who knew blooms could take to flight?

Dancing in circles, a floral tease,
Making ants do the jive with ease.
Nature's own stand-up, catch their show,
With jokes only the flowers know!

Cherry Kisses in the Warmth of the Sun

Sunbeams tickle, oh what a game,
Flower faces, all without shame.
They blush and giggle, it's quite absurd,
A comedy of colors, haven't you heard?

Bumblebees wear shades, feeling cool,
Wind whispers jokes, nature's own fool.
With smiles and snickers, all in a whirl,
Spring's vibrant humor begins to unfurl!

Delicate Sentinels of the Season

Tiny petals dance, oh so spry,
In a breeze that tickles, they flutter high.
Whispers of spring on a sunbeam ride,
Pretending to be shy but bursting with pride.

They nod to bumblebees with a laugh,
Unfurling their charms as if on behalf.
A giggle here, a chuckle there,
Spreading sweet mischief—breathe in their flair.

Nature's Quiet Revelations

In the garden, secrets bloom,
Each with a grin, dispelling gloom.
Poking through soil, they conspire and play,
Bringing joy to the start of the day.

Their blooms wear laughter, not a care,
Stealing sunshine, unaware of their flair.
They tease the clouds to come join in,
Nature's own jesters, ready to win!

Where Beauty Sways with the Breeze

Watch how they sway, those dainty dreams,
Twirling to tunes, or so it seems.
Whirling in circles, oh what a sight,
Making the world feel ever so light.

They shimmer and shake, in jovial cheer,
Sending quiet giggles, oh so near.
With every soft gust, a joke is found,
Nature's own dance, spinning all around.

The Call of the Awakening Flora

Listen closely, a chorus begins,
Nature's pranksters, where laughter spins.
With each new bud, a story is told,
Of droll adventures, both brave and bold.

A splash of color, a wink in the light,
They glitter with mischief, a pure delight.
Tickling the earth with their playful flair,
Awakening joy like spring in the air.

The Symphony of Beauty Unfolding

A swirl of color in the wind,
Bees buzzing, oh what a din!
Flowers giggle, petals flip,
Nature's stage, a lively trip.

Grass plays flute, the trees on beat,
Squirrels dance, they can't be beat!
The sun joins in, a warming ray,
As laughter fills this bloom-filled play.

A Daydream Cloaked in Floral Hues.

In a land where blossoms reign,
I lost my sock, could it be plain?
They tiptoe on the breezy stage,
While I try hard to save my page.

A butterfly mocks my frantic run,
Her flight is graceful, mine is fun!
I trip on roots with quite a dash,
These days are silly—what a splash!

Whispers of Spring's Gentle Embrace

The wind tells jokes, a teasing breeze,
It tickles me like playful fleece.
Flowers wink with a cheeky grin,
As squirrels wear their hats of skin!

Oh, how the daisies gossip loud!
They giggle, shrug, then call a crowd.
While I sip tea from my own cup,
They slide and tumble, what a sup!

Petals Dance on the Breeze

Look at the leaves doing the twist,
They seem to know the steps we missed.
A ladybug sings a tune so bright,
While ants march in with sheer delight.

We join the party, a motley crew,
With flower hats and a grand new view.
A picnic starts where bees wear ties,
And laughter soars into the skies.

Clouds of Petal Confetti

Dancing flakes from above,
Like nature's silly joke,
They twirl and spin with glee,
Laughing as they soak.

A bee wearing a hat,
Waves to a passing snail,
With petals as their pass,
They set off on a trail.

The sun peeks through the storm,
A giggle here, a cheer,
While squirrels play charades,
And squirrels just disappear.

In a tumble of pink,
The earth laughs with delight,
Confetti in the breeze,
What a wacky sight!

Beneath the Canopy of Spring's Tears

A droplet falls like laughter,
Splat, right on my nose,
It's nature's heavy chuckle,
As muddy pants now pose.

Umbrellas pop like mushrooms,
As rainclouds start to play,
We jump in every puddle,
In spring's own cabaret.

A frog sings on a lily,
With a voice loud and deep,
As toads start bouncing round,
It's a wet hop and leap.

Under weeping willows,
Where raindrops lightly tease,
The trees join in with giggles,
And sway a little breeze.

The Breath of New Beginnings

A breeze whispers gently,
Is it me or the trees?
Inhale the jokes of spring,
With a side of allergies.

New shoots pop their heads up,
Awkward and quite bold,
They stumble on their roots,
Like stories yet untold.

With ladybugs applauding,
And ants in suits parade,
Tiny comedy shows,
In the bright sunshine displayed.

Each bud seems to quip,
As they unfurl with zest,
Nature's comedy club,
In bloom, it feels like a fest!

Singing with the Melodic Wind

The wind hums a jolly tune,
As trees dance to the beat,
A gust fluffs up my hair,
And sweeps me off my feet.

Quacking ducks join in song,
With a splash and a quack,
They waddle with such style,
No thought of looking back.

The daisies start to giggle,
With petals all askew,
"Oh dear, what's a flower's style?
Just laugh and bloom anew!"

Together, under sunshine,
We dance 'til we're tired,
In the silly symphony,
Of springtime, we are inspired!

The Lure of Early Morning Blossoms

In the dawn, petals prance,
Bees in a silly dance,
Buzzing round like they're in jest,
Searching for their pollen quest.

Coffee spills while I attempt,
To admire nature's pretense,
A breeze blows through with an aim,
Not knowing I'm late for the game.

The sun peeks with a cheeky grin,
While birds argue who'll sing first in,
I laugh at the chaos unfurled,
Morning mischief wakes the world.

With each bloom, a strike of fate,
Nature's joke, can't be too late,
Life's a giggle, full of cheer,
In springtime's laughter, we adhere.

Kaleidoscope of Floral Dreams

Petals tumble, colors spin,
In morning's light, where dreams begin,
Leaves wave like they know the score,
They're telling secrets, who could ignore?

Bumblebees load up on their stash,
Like tiny trucks in a floral dash,
Oh, to be a bloom for a day,
Where worries melt, and puns play.

Butterflies in a dizzy whirl,
Flutter around for a fun twirl,
Who knew that they'd dance so bold?
In this garden, watch stories unfold.

Nature's circus, come one, come all,
Where mischief's the language of the call,
With a giggle in every petal's sway,
Life's a joke, let's laugh our way.

Subtle Hues in the Light's Embrace

Bright hues fight for the spotlight,
Under the sun, they claim their right,
A blush here, a wink there,
Who said a flower can't wear flair?

In the breeze, they twist and twine,
Like they're rehearsing for a line,
Swaying to a nature song,
Who knew it'd get so silly along?

Colors clash in a playful feud,
Roses pouting, violets rude,
A poppy giggles, quite the scene,
In their world, I've never been keen.

But oh, how they make me smile,
In their company, I could stay a while,
The sun's rays tickle every petal,
In this laugh, our hearts settle.

A Gentle Rain of Petals

When petals fall like confetti,
The ground laughs, oh so ready,
Dancing down in a bright mishap,
Like nature's own quirky wrap.

With each step, a soft squish sound,
Who knew such joy could be found?
The prancing squirrels stop to stare,
In awe of this floral affair.

A leaf slips past, what a jest,
Nature's prank, oh, she knows best,
The blue sky chuckles in delight,
What a show, what a sight!

So, let it rain, this floral gift,
In the giggles, we all drift,
Life's a party in petals' play,
Join the dance, come what may!

Whispers of Spring's Bloom

Tiny petals giggle loud,
As the wind twists like a crowd.
Squirrels dance on branches high,
While sneezing bees just flutter by.

Buds play hide and seek with light,
Tickling noses, oh what a sight!
A dancing twig, a laughing sprout,
Springtime jokes we can't live without.

Butterflies wear silly hats,
As they chase chubby, funny cats.
Blooming laughter fills the air,
Spreading smiles, without a care.

Petals Dancing in the Breeze

Whirling petals spin and twirl,
The squirrels chase in a leafy whirl.
Like little fairies lost in play,
They tease the sunlight every day.

A flower's wink, a bee's quick laugh,
As feathers float a silly gaffe.
Trees nod their heads with glee and flair,
While grasshoppers jump without a care.

Breezy jokes that tickle our necks,
While chubby ladybugs seek their checks.
A bumblebee with mischief's quest,
Pollinates while taking a rest.

Fragrance of the Awakening

The scent of laughter fills the air,
As petals wiggle everywhere.
Fragrant jests on a morning stroll,
Playful air, tickling the soul.

A dandelion turns to jest,
Making wishes, never unrest.
Blossoms giggle at skies so blue,
Delighted in their playful view.

The thunderous roar of sleepy bees,
Awakens dreams in the gentle breeze.
Misty whispers from blooms so sweet,
Funny tales dance at our feet.

Joyful Secrets in the Wind

Secrets swirl like candy fluff,
While blossoms tease with playful puff.
Giggling petals share a grin,
As chasing raindrops dash about and spin.

The wind knows jokes, a merry trick,
As breezes tease with laughter thick.
Each rustling leaf whispers a song,
Enticing us to join along.

A butterfly flirts, then takes flight,
While a worm looks on with delight.
Nature's pranksters, all in play,
Blooming laughter guides our way.

Scented Echoes of New Beginnings

In the garden, scents collide,
Wobbly bees take a goofy ride.
Petals laugh, they dance around,
Sprightly whispers, joy is found.

Giggling trees, what a sight,
Winks from buds, oh what delight!
A bumble's stumble, a butterfly's cheer,
Nature's jesters, bringing good cheer.

A Symphony of Pink and White

In the breeze, hues play nice,
A ballet of color, oh how precise!
With every flutter, jokes they tell,
A symphony bright, ringing like a bell.

Here comes Mr. Ant on a spree,
Twisting and turning, thinking he's free!
A slippery branch, oh what a fall,
Laughter echoes, nature's own call.

Dancing Petals on the Canvas of Sky

Petals twirl, not one is shy,
Painting clouds as they drift by.
A cheeky wind gives them a shove,
They giggle and sway, it's the dance they love.

Birds in tuxedos chirp in tune,
While worms throw parties beneath the moon.
A painter's palette gone slightly mad,
Cheerful chaos, it's just too rad!

Blossoms on the Breath of Nature

Nature sneezed, and flowers bloomed,
What a mess, oh how they zoomed!
With pollen tickles and fragrant flair,
They giggle softly, beyond compare.

In the meadows, baby buds play,
Trading whispers on sunny days.
With a wink and a twist, they sway just right,
Eager to conquer the warm sunlight.

Serene Harmonies of Fragile Beauty

In the garden, a dance of cheer,
Tiny petals whisper quite near.
They sway and twirl in the breeze,
Tickling noses, oh what a tease!

Laughter erupts as they float,
Caught on a silly hat, they gloat.
A bee buzzes with a charming grin,
Sipping nectar, let the fun begin!

A breeze comes by, a sudden swoosh,
Caught off guard, we all just whoosh.
Like confetti in a playful show,
Nature's prankster, putting on quite a glow!

Amidst the joy, a stork takes a peek,
Wondering if this flower's the peak.
Like sending a postcard from a trip,
Nature's humor, oh what a quip!

Petals Alight on Spring's Finger

Spring arrives with giggles and grins,
As petals play tricks on our chins.
They land on dogs, they whirl and dive,
Making each moment come alive!

Birds chirp out, a playful tune,
Reciting rhymes about the moon.
One flower tickles a passing cat,
The chase ensues - oh, imagine that!

Butterflies join in the spree,
Twisting and turning, oh so free.
Landing on hats, hats off they fly,
Nature's jests will never die!

As laughter lingers in the air,
We dance like petals without a care.
All around, the world's in bloom,
With giggles and fun, there's never gloom!

Reveries of Crescent Blooms

In dreamy fields where giggles grow,
Crescent colors start the show.
Dancing together, they bring delight,
Swirling and twirling, what a sight!

A playful breeze with a cheeky grin,
Looks for trouble, let the games begin!
Petals on toes, they hop and prance,
Who knew flowers could dance?

Squirrels join in with a bounce,
Chasing petals, what a flounce!
With acorns flying, laughter rings,
While nature plays with all these things.

In the sky, clouds giggle too,
They puff and billow, oh, what a view!
The world's a stage of color and flair,
Where every petal bursts with flair!

Traces of Color in the Morning Mist

Morning mist plays a light-hearted game,
Dressing each flower, never the same.
Silly shadows peek out and sway,
As creatures of whimsy come out to play!

Charming aromas rise and twirl,
Chasing critters in a joyful whirl.
A ladybug dons a flower hat,
Strolling proudly, oh, imagine that!

Frogs leap into the puddles near,
Splashing colors, they cheer and cheer!
A syncopated rhythm they confess,
Nature's spree, we're all in jest!

With laughter echoing in every nook,
Dreams blend with joy, let's take a look.
In each petal, a tale anew,
In this playful world, anything will do!

Fragile Beauty in Gentle Gales

Petals flutter like kittens in flight,
Bouncing off noses with all of their might.
Whispers of spring tickle our ears,
While pollen forms sneeze attacks, oh dear!

Trees dressed in lace, oh what a delight,
With blossoms that giggle in morning light.
As bees do the cha-cha on each branch,
They seem to be waiting for their big chance.

A breeze comes along, sends them in a twirl,
Like flighty dancers who just love to whirl.
Laughter erupts with each bloom's little shake,
Nature's own jester, make no mistake!

So let's chase these fluffs on this fine sunny day,
With jokes in our pockets, let's laugh all the way.
For in this floral circus, joy's everywhere,
A whimsical show in the fragrant fresh air.

A Tapestry of Floral Dreams

In gardens where laughter plays hide and seek,
Colors parade, and the blossoms all squeak.
Petals may giggle, and leaves start to sway,
A silly display in this flowery ballet.

The bees wear their sunglasses, strut with great flair,
While ladybugs gossip, without any care.
A jolly old hedgehog joins in the fun,
He twirls on a leaf, like he's just begun.

Blooming comedians play tricks on the sun,
Casting long shadows, making fun of the run.
Dandelions puff with pride on the scene,
As if they're the stars of a wild magazine.

So let's frolic through blooms, with laughter so bright,
In this floral fiesta, our spirits take flight.
With whimsical patterns woven in air,
Nature's own tapestry leads without care.

Celestial Blooms Beneath a Soft Sky

Clouds wear a coat of cotton candy pride,
As blossoms below twist and giggle with stride.
The sun plays peek-a-boo with flowers in line,
While critters crack jokes for a glass of sunshine.

A butterfly flirts, a connoisseur of grace,
While daisies remark with a charming embrace.
"Dressed like a prom queen, all this fuss for me?"
A madcap adventure beneath the sky's spree.

In this grand merriment, laughter cascades,
Each petal a story that never fades.
"Let's serve up a brunch!" the lilacs do chirp,
"On pancakes of pollen, let's giggle and burp!"

So linger awhile in this whimsical air,
Where humor and beauty make quite a rare pair.
As celestial blooms sway in soft, swirling light,
Nature's own giggles will carry the night.

The Dance of Graceful Blooms

A jester of colors upon the green stage,
They twirl and they leap, defying their age.
With each gentle gust, they whirl and they spin,
Nature's funny show, let the laughter begin!

A waltz of the buds in a breezy parade,
While tulips throw shade, decked in flamboyant jade.
They giggle and sway, a floral charade,
With whispers of mischief in every cascade.

The daisies make jokes with the wind as it howls,
While marigolds chuckle and roll like a fowl.
"Who tripped on the roots? Oh dear, what a sight!"
In this dance of blooms, the world feels so right.

Come join in this jest, where laughter will bloom,
In gardens of giggles, dispelling all gloom.
For when petals are dancing, the heart can't resist,
A merry affair, in nature's sweet tryst.

Blossoms Tied to Dreams of Tomorrow

Floating petals dance in glee,
As they plot their great escape,
They giggle on the gentle breeze,
Wearing their floral capes.

Little critters join the fray,
A bee shows off its fancy spin,
While ants parade in grand ballet,
Chasing after sweet divine sin.

A wish is tossed on lemon skies,
Tickled by a cheeky breeze,
Where each flower wears a guise,
Dreaming of worlds like fluffy cheese.

In a whirl of color bright,
Nature's jest, a playful sight,
They laugh as spring begins to bloom,
Transforming gloom into a room.

Resilience in the Face of the Wind

Oh, merry buds with spunky flair,
Laugh while wind tries to test your might,
With wobbly dances, you'll declare,
"You can't blow out our joyful light!"

Dandelions puff and peer around,
Swaying like they're at a ball,
Their laughter rises, soft yet sound,
While winds stomp and try to enthrall.

Twisting and turning, they won't fall,
Their petals tickled, just a tease,
Shouting, 'Hey, we're having a ball!"
While wind lays down its own unease.

With every gust, they've learned to sway,
And giggle as the world spins round,
For springtime blooms don't shy away,
They always leap back from the ground.

Echoes of Joy Beneath the Trees

Beneath the branches, giggles rise,
As critters host their secret shows,
With acorn hats and twinkling eyes,
They weave a tale that nobody knows.

Squirrels perform in choreographed leaps,
While birds chirp, the orchestra plays,
Nature's laughter softly creeps,
Through rustling leaves on sunny days.

A dance-off sprouts on cozy grass,
Where each plant shakes its leafy boots,
And shadows swirl as moments pass,
Creating funky, leafy hoots.

As echoes of joy bounce all around,
Trees whisper secrets, laughter flows,
In this haven beneath the ground,
Where every heart is free to pose.

The Silent Language of Vibrant Hues

Colors chat in whispers sly,
As vivid shades make faces glow,
Crimson winks, while yellow sighs,
And blues strut like a fashion show.

They gossip through the sunlit beams,
"Look at us, we're quite the crew!"
In garden corners, paint their dreams,
While grasses play peek-a-boo.

Lavender's humor is quite bizarre,
"Try to catch us if you can!"
As petals roll beneath the star,
Flirting thus, with nature's plan.

In a palette of giggles and cheer,
The silent talks unfold with grace,
As nature's hues whisper near,
With every twist, they embrace.

Threads of Pink in the Velvet Sky

In springtime's jest, the colors dance,
A rosy prank in every glance.
Cherry giggles cross the breeze,
Tickling noses with such ease.

Fluffy clouds play hide and seek,
While petals wiggle, ever cheek.
Laughing trees sway in delight,
Nature's jesters, what a sight!

Bumblebees join in the fun,
Buzzing loudly, here they run.
With pollen dusting, shoes overdue,
They dance a jig, a merry crew.

So if you find your heart too gray,
Just look for pink, come out and play.
Nature's humor fills the air,
In laughter's bloom, we all can share.

A Garden of Ephemeral Delights

In gardens full of giggles bright,
Petals gossip in sunlight.
Butterflies, dressed to impress,
Flirt and flutter, nothing less.

Bees in suits, they buzz around,
Spilling jokes on fertile ground.
Every blossom lends a grin,
With nature's laughter, we all win.

Twirling vines in playful spins,
Planting seeds of silly sins.
Sprouts of humor bloom so rare,
In this garden, love is air.

Laughter sprouts from every shoot,
As squirrels dance in pursuit.
Chasing tails in silly fights,
Nature's jesters, sweet delights.

Nature's Caress in Gentle Breezes

A gentle breeze, a playful touch,
Whispers softly, oh so much.
It carries secrets, silly tales,
Of fluttering wings and tiny snails.

Swaying branches giggle light,
With every sway, they spark delight.
The daisies wink, the daisies nudge,
Nature laughs, we can't begrudge.

Clouds overhead, like puffy sheep,
Bouncing gently, oh so sweet.
The sun winks down, a cheeky star,
As butterflies dance near and far.

Oh, breathe it in, this quirky air,
A joyful twist everywhere.
With every laugh, the world's a cheer,
Nature smiles, and we draw near.

Hanging Sweets in the Warm Spring Air

Sweet treats dangle from each branch,
A candy land with every chance.
Jellybeans peek out to say,
"Come on! Let's have fun today!"

Syrup drips from every flower,
Sucking nectar, hour by hour.
Bees become the party crew,
Mixing up the sweet with dew.

With gummy worms that twist and twirl,
Nature's sweets make our heads whirl.
Sipping sunshine, tasting cheer,
Springtime whispers, "Come on near!"

So if you crave a bit of fun,
Join the frolic, it's just begun.
With laughter heard, and sweets to share,
The world is bright, and joy is rare.

A Mosaic of Short-lived Grace

Amidst the branches, giggles play,
Little blooms sway, bright and gay.
Nature's confetti, a cheeky tease,
Whispering secrets with every breeze.

In a parade, they dance and spin,
A jolly fiesta where laughter begins.
Petals fall like jokes from the skies,
Leaving behind quirky goodbyes.

A flower's crown on a squirrel's head,
He struts around, proud instead.
"Oh, I'm the king!" he seems to say,
As blooms float down in a playful way.

Just watch the bees; they hum and buzz,
With pollen stashes, they create a fuzz.
They trip and tumble, like silly clowns,
Gathering laughter from floral crowns.

Echoes of Petals in the Twilight

In evening glow, they flutter and flit,
Like tiny dancers keen to commit.
With a wobbly grace, they twirl in glee,
Sprinkling chuckles like stardust free.

Chasing shadows, they giggle away,
Skipping on whispers of the day.
As crickets chirp their evening song,
Petals join in, where they belong.

A broomstick for a beetle, oh what a sight!
With wings spread wide, he takes to flight.
"Dance with me, friends!" he bravely shouts,
While petals giggle, spinning about.

End-of-day parties, nature's ball,
Each fluttering prank, a delightful sprawl.
They tell the tales of joy and cheer,
In the twilight air, where laughter's near.

Graceful Formations of Soft Pink

Soft pinks gather, a cotton candy crew,
They wiggle and laugh as the breezes blew.
"Oh no, watch out!" cries a hapless bee,
As blossoms giggle, falling free.

An accidental shower of petals on heads,
Turning folks into flower-seated spreads.
"Decorate me!" says a nearby cat,
As flowers blanket him, chitchat and chat.

They whisper jokes with a twinkling glee,
"What's the best color?" in playful decree.
"Why, pink of course, it's all the rage!"
As blooms burst forth, they center stage.

Silly stories are sewn in the air,
With blossoms laughing, they have no care.
In formations, they tumble, giggling about,
Creating hilarity when in full rout.

Nature's Tiny Perfumed Fireworks

Puffing and popping, like mini bombs,
Sprays of fragrance, oh how it calms.
In bursts of color, they light the night,
With laughter echoing, oh what a sight!

Squirrels take cover, unsure what to make,
Of explosions of pink, for goodness' sake!
"Is it raining blooms?" one starling cried,
While petals bounced like children, with pride.

"Look out below!" shouts a clumsy dove,
As blossoms flutter, a sign of love.
Fireworks of nature, in a playful spree,
Celebrating life with floral glee.

In a flash, they twirl, in soft starlit air,
With each little drop, they kiddingly flare.
A joke of creation, so funny and spry,
With petals dancing, they catch your eye.

Yearning in the Flutter of Wings

Little birds chase dreams, so bright,
In a dance that's quite a delight,
They whisper sweet secrets to the trees,
And giggle at bees with wobbly knees.

They flutter and flap in grand ballet,
Creating a mess in a feathery way,
With each twist and turn, they try to impress,
But land in the wrong nest, oh what a mess!

A squirrel rolls by, not sure what to do,
Tripping on branches, oh who'd ever knew?
He stares at the sky, and then at the ground,
And laughs at the chaos that's all around.

So here we gather, with hearts full of cheer,
Watching these antics, we all disappear,
Laughter erupts, as we join in the fun,
In this whimsical world, we dance in the sun.

The Art of Petals Falling Softly

Petals pirouette from their lofty place,
With grace that has captured, the world's embrace,
They tumble and spin, a laugh in the breeze,
Tickling the noses of snoozing trees.

One silly blossom, with antics quite grand,
Floats down to rest, on an unsuspecting hand,
The owner jumps up, aghast at the sight,
It's just nature's jest, oh what pure delight!

Breezy jesters in a floral parade,
Causing mischief wherever they've laid,
A petal-army of short-lived glee,
Cheering us all to partake and be free.

So let's raise a toast, to the merry display,
For moments like these, we'll laugh all day,
With petals around, and joy in the air,
Life's little jokes are beyond compare.

Bright Horizons Above the Blossoms

The sun stretches wide, a golden crown,
Chasing away the sleepy town,
Blooms smile up, with giggles of light,
As butterflies stumble, what a funny sight!

They fumble and flop, like they've lost their map,
Bumping into petals, wheezing a laugh,
Their dance is a riddle, a comical spree,
Colors collide, what a sight to see!

A noodle of wind, tickles the air,
Sending them spinning, without a care,
And as they twirl, they forget their grace,
A tumble, a roll, and then a trace!

With chuckles abound, we bask in the glow,
Under blossoms that sprinkle, the world with a show,
So here's to the comedy, life has in store,
With each blooming joke, who could ask for more?

Surrender to the Soft Caress of Nature

The gentle hush of a whispering breeze,
Entices us all like a simmering tease,
With faces upturned, we giggle and sway,
Nature's warm hug brightens up our day.

Softly it beckons, the grass and the flowers,
Inviting us in for some playful hours,
But a bee zooms by, in a frantic chase,
Sending us diving, a silly embrace!

A dandelion puffs, like a puffed-up fool,
Sprinkling its seeds, making laughter the rule,
As children erupt with squeals of pure joy,
Chasing the fluff, oh what a ploy!

So let us surrender, to moments of play,
In nature's warm arms, we'll laugh all the way,
For underneath skies, where humor is found,
We revel in peace, and joy all around.

Tender Moments in Nature's Gallery

In spring, the petals take a dive,
A sneaky wind helps them arrive.
They tickle noses, oh what a game,
Nature's pranks, never the same.

A squirrel sneezes, a bird takes flight,
Whispers of laughter, pure delight.
They dance like confetti, oh what a show,
Getting all giggly, as breezes blow.

A bee buzzes loudly, acts quite a fool,
Pollinate here? No, let's just drool!
He trips on a petal, tumbles around,
Nature's comedy, love it unbound!

With every bloom, a new joke unfolds,
Silly antics, stories retold.
Even the sun wears a smile so bright,
In this playground, fun is the sight.

The Scent of Life in Bloom

Whiffs of sweetness drift through the air,
A flower's perfume, beyond compare.
A bee in a tux, what a fancy guest,
Buzzing and swirling, he's on a quest.

Grass tickles toes with a playful tease,
While clovers giggle, swaying in ease.
The ants hold a party, snacks galore,
But someone forgot to lock the door!

A ladybug dines on crumbs from cake,
And a snail says, slow down for goodness' sake!
With scents of life, and laughter so bright,
Nature's humor hits the highest height.

Each blossom a joke, each breeze a cheer,
In this fragrant world, joy is near.
So come take a whiff, let your worries zoom,
In the garden of laughter, the air's in full bloom!

Dancers in the Soft Light

Sunbeams twirl like dancers in play,
Light winks and whispers, 'Hey, come this way!'
Petals shimmy on branches so tall,
As shadows pirouette, giving their all.

A butterfly tripped on his own little wing,
Did a flip and fell, what a silly thing!
Laughter erupted among the bright leaves,
Nature's ballet, oh how it weaves!

Frogs leap and croak, as beats catch the air,
While the leaves join in, swaying with flair.
Grasshoppers jump in choreographed rows,
Even the groundhog shows off his toes!

The moon peeks in, gives a cheeky grin,
With stars all clapping, let's all begin!
In this dance of glee, join the delight,
For every soft moment, is magic in flight.

Fluttering Colors of Seasonal Change

Oh look at the colors, spinning and swirled,
A canvas of nature, so boldly unfurled.
Leaves red and gold, in a funny parade,
While squirrels squirrel away, their plans they made.

The wind tosses leaves like confetti in play,
Who's the DJ? It's nature today!
They shimmied and shook, as if on a spree,
Turning the ground into a vibrant sea.

A crow thinks he's cool, struts about with flair,
Trying to steal all the attention there.
But the colors just laugh, they shine and they twirl,
While the crow takes a tumble – oh what a whirl!

With each blustery gust, the party goes wild,
Nature chuckles softly, like a mischievous child.
In a riot of colors, loud laughs will ring,
Celebrating change, let the fun begin!

Lullabies of Cherry Scent

In the breeze, they pirouette,
Frolicking with a floral threat.
Bees complain, oh what a tease,
Dancing lightly on the knees.

Sticking to each passerby,
A pink surprise, oh my oh my!
Squirrels giggle, they can't resist,
A feast in fragrance, just like this.

Birds tumble in flowery dreams,
Tickling tails and cheeky schemes.
While the trees wear silly grins,
Laughing where the fun begins.

Petals prance and twirl with flair,
Causing joy, beyond compare.
Who knew spring could be so spry?
With scents that tickle, oh me, oh my!

Secrets Written in the Petal's Dance

A waltzing bud begins to yak,
Whispers float, then take a crack.
Leaves eavesdrop on every twirl,
Caught up in all the floral whirl.

Petals giggle, share a jest,
Nature's humor, always best.
They spin tales of the winged bee,
And plot against the sleepy tree.

With every gust, they sway and sway,
In a game of hide and play.
Laughter muffled, but so clear,
Who knew flowers could be such peers?

Every dance step hides a quirk,
While sunshine spills, they start to smirk.
Secrets bloom in pure delight,
Nature's giggles, what a sight!

Enchanted Whispers of Nature's Palette

Strokes of color, errant glee,
Swaying softly, wild and free.
Nature's palette, splashes bright,
Doodling joy from morn to night.

Green giggles as the blues collide,
While yellows grin and take a ride.
With paints that spill, oh what a mess,
Creating chaos—who would guess?

Daisies blush and sunflowers beam,
As petals dance in laughter's theme.
Brushes dipped in spring's embrace,
Create a smile on every face.

Oh, the colors sing a tune,
Under the watchful, jolly moon.
Each hue a chuckle, light and rare,
In the art of joy—beyond compare!

The Art of Seasonal Embrace

Winter chuckles as spring is near,
Bidding farewell with frosty cheer.
Snowflakes yearn for warmer days,
As sunshine draws in giggling rays.

Spring arrives with playful prance,
Each bloom joins the happy dance.
Trees wear coats of vibrant hues,
Nature offers up her clues.

The sun beams bright, a cheeky mime,
Chasing shadows, having a time.
With every raindrop, a splash of fun,
Laughter echoes, spring has begun!

From the ground, the green sprouts rise,
Tickling ankles, much to our surprise.
Nature's jesters, in bloom so bold,
Spring and winter—comedy untold!

A Breath of Floral Serenity

In the breeze, petals fly,
Tickling noses without a sigh,
Bees are buzzing with such delight,
Honey's coming, what a sight!

Squirrels dance beneath the tree,
Chasing shadows, wild and free,
A dog sneezes, what a scene,
A laugh erupts, full of green!

Worms wiggle, making their way,
Underneath the ground, they play,
The sun peeks in, a grin so bright,
Nature's joke, pure delight!

So if you wander where it's fair,
Join the fun, breathe in the air,
Forget your worries, let them go,
Life's a joke, enjoy the show!

Velvet Whispers of Springtime Grace

Softly giggles in the mist,
Fluffy clouds that can't resist,
A ladybug upon a leaf,
Sipping nectar, oh so brief!

Frogs in chorus sing their song,
Ribbit, ribbit, all day long,
While butterflies, in grand parade,
Flap their wings, a funny charade!

Buds are blushing on the vine,
Cheeky blooms, oh how they shine,
A bumblebee with silly flair,
Buzzing around without a care!

So take a moment, stop and stare,
Nature's laughter's everywhere,
In every petal, leaf and sound,
Joy and humor can be found!

Chasing the Colors of the Wind

Colorful kites, they dance and soar,
Windy whispers, oh what a chore,
But giggles spill from little mouths,
As laughter twirls, joy unshrouds!

Grasshoppers hop, they plot and plan,
To steal a snack from picnic's span,
While ants march like a tiny band,
In search of crumbs, oh isn't that grand?

Clouds wear hats, fluffy and white,
Winking down, what a silly sight,
Trees wave gladly, proud and tall,
Join the fun, come one, come all!

So let the wind play tricks today,
Chase those colors, come what may,
For in this dance of nature's play,
There's laughter brightening the day!

Serenade of Blooming Laughter

In the garden, giggles bloom,
Petals chuckle, sparing gloom,
A twist of vine, a playful hug,
Nature's pranks, all quite snug!

Chirping birds with silly songs,
Hop on branches, where it belongs,
A cat yawns, looks quite bemused,
While bees buzz softly, all confused!

Dandelions wear their crowns,
Puffed up like fluffy, cheerful clowns,
A breeze swirls in, tickling all,
Even grumpy trees start to sprawl!

So let's celebrate with a cheer,
For springtime's antics, oh so dear,
In every bloom, and every laugh,
Life's a funny, fragrant path!

www.ingramcontent.com/pod-product-compliance
Lightning Source LLC
Chambersburg PA
CBHW060146230426
43661CB00003B/593